Gnostic Models

Thinking About Embodiment

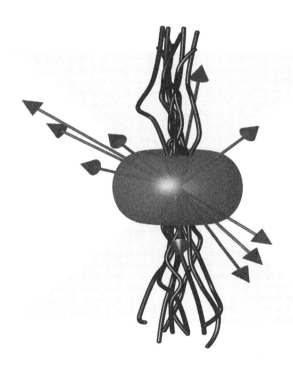

Gnostic Models

Thinking About Embodiment

ArborRhythms Publishing
Ashland, OR

Title: Gnostic Models

Subtitle: Thinking About Embodiment

Author: Alec M Rogers

URL: http://GnosticModels.com

ISBN: 978-098-303765-1

Library of Congress
Control Number: 2022909081

Revision 0.9: April 29th, 2022
Revision 1.0: June 21st, 2022

Dedication

This book is dedicated to truth.

*May it be spoken everywhere
and bring joy to those that hear it.*

Preface

Self-models form a basis for thinking, feeling, and acting in the world: the better our models are, the better we know and navigate reality. Although models of reality are often more highly valued than models of the self, we cannot form a good model of reality unless we also have a good model of the mind that builds that model of reality. So who and what are we? And precisely where and when are we?

At least superficially, the answers to these questions are familiar: we each comprise a 3-D physical body that knows various concepts and feels various emotions. But do our models accurately correspond to the feeling of being embodied, and do they encapsulate the wisdom of our emotions? To dispel any limiting beliefs about who we are, this work explores several multidimensional models of mind, emotions, and body.

Table of Contents

PART I

INTRODUCTION

Gnostic models are mental models. This is meant in two ways: they are models of our mind and they are models that our mind uses.

If we do not have a model of the mind that we use to understand the world, we are likely to become confused by projecting aspects of our mind onto physical reality. For example, should our suffering be understood as a result of our mind or the world? Models allow us to examine this question with precision, and thereby to deepen our knowledge.

Gnostic models are also models that our mind uses. We would not move without emotions, and we could not move without bodies. However, accurate *models* of emotions, bodies, and the profound wisdom they represent are fundamental for correctly interpreting our sensations and thus for living well.

1. Models

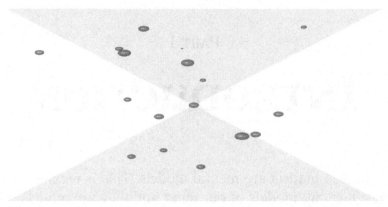

Figure 1: A spacetime diagram showing scattered events.

1.1 *Gnosis*

Gnosis literally means knowledge, but it connotes knowing oneself or building a model of oneself. Knowing oneself is so important that people have seen gnosis as a technique of spiritual liberation since at least the time of ancient Greece; in fact, "Know thyself" was inscribed at the entrance to the temple of Apollo.[1] But whether gnosis brings liberation or not, knowing how the world works and how our mind works allows us to be happier and more embodied. For example, if we think that objects in the world are permanent, then we will be unhappily surprised when things break. So what should we do about that? One response is to model everything as impermanent, although it's also helpful to understand why we initially thought that everything was permanent.

Gnostic models help us perform meta-level analyses of our own experience. Based on those analyses, we can be more equanimous and think more efficiently. However, working with a model requires observing the mind and defining somewhat precisely what feelings and thoughts are, which is difficult since feelings and thoughts are not shared experiences. Therefore, even though models of feeling and thought inevitably oversimplify the phenomena they describe, they are necessary to conduct meta-analyses of feeling and thinking.

1.2 *Cultural Transmission*

The strategies that we use to navigate in the world are often learned implicitly from language and culture, so we do not necessarily have corresponding models of those strategies. For example, we all learn language, but we do not all learn linguistic theory or how our words relate to the world. Since languages have structures that subtly but systematically distort reality, each new generation is apt to misunderstand reality unless we provide an explicit model. Even if we are actively engaged in training our bodies and minds, the subjective mental models our society provides are often inadequate compared to its rather elaborate models of technology and other objective phenomena.

It is particularly important to provide excellent (subjective) mental models of experience since they are required to understand physical models. For example, because our mind determines how we perceive and conceptualize the world, we might act as if the world was discrete simply because our thoughts are discrete. On the other hand, if we have a model of our mind as discrete, it allows us to experience the continuity of the world better by recognizing and removing any aspects of our minds that we have accidentally projected onto reality. In this way, models often point beyond themselves: while we might use models to understand continuity, our interaction with the world may need to be model-free if we truly want to operate smoothly.

1.3 *The Lump Model*

Modeling our self is difficult because the subjective point of view cannot be intersubjectively verified. For example, when we talk about what something feels like, we communicate our thoughts rather than our feelings, and the gap between those two is extremely significant. However, there are numerous characteristics of human minds that we can model, and such modeling may help us to overcome systematic biases that result from our shared mental structures.

The most simple self-model is the Lump Model, which describes the self as a single unit that fuses the mental, emotional, and physical aspects of the self.[2] Language and culture implicitly reinforce this model by using the personal pronoun "I" or by treating humans as individual legal entities. While the Lump Model is convenient, it is not sufficient and is often problematic. In particular, modeling ourselves as isolated units rather than embodied or interconnected beings is often accompanied by alienation from the world, selfishness, and confusion. Abandoning the Lump Model clarifies two significant mistakes: mistaking the location of the body as the location of the mind and mistaking the location of the mind as the location of the body.

1.4 *The Map and Vehicle Model*

The Map and Vehicle Model describes the mind as a map and describes awareness as a vehicle that is driven over that map, where the headlights of the vehicle help us see the dark terrain. Although the Map and Vehicle Model is a relatively simple model of cognition, it adds an important level of meta-analysis that allows us to think about the mind itself, rather than using the mind to think about other objects.

As an example of working with a mental model, suppose we perceive a wooden chair. Although it is possible to be aware of the content of our concepts about that chair, such as how comfortable the chair is, we can also use the Map and Vehicle model to be *aware of the awareness* of the chair. At that meta-level, we are aware of the vehicle rather than being directly aware of the chair. That abstraction facilitates knowing things about awareness such as its size or its velocity as our attention shifts from one object to another, rather than knowing things about the chair itself.

Thus, a mental model allows us to create maps of maps, or to represent our awareness at a meta-level. Ultimately, that may enable awareness at a *lower* level: for example, thinking about the movement of our awareness might help us to feel that movement in space, a sensation that does not inherently require any meta-analysis. Feeling that movement is a significant step in becoming embodied and has several benefits as compared to thinking about thinking.

2. The Self Model

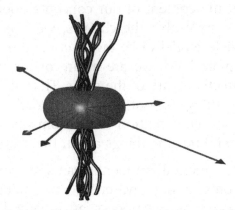

Figure 2: A model depicting mind, emotions, and body.

2.1 *Who Am I?*

Self-models make our behavior more explicit. Thus, developing models of ourselves allows us to become more skillful. For example, they allow us to identify and abandon implicit models such as the Lump Model that are often counterproductive. However, knowing what we need to model is nontrivial; each of us begins with a different implicit model, so we each need to learn different things. Ultimately, however, our disparate models converge as they collect an increasing amount of truth.

Gnostic models can be categorized into three main types according to their perspective or point of view: subjective, objective, and physical. *Subjective Models* are the models by which each of us understands our world, and which correspond to our subjective points of view. The *Objective Model* is the intersection of what is true from every subjective point of view; it is the domain of science. The *Physical Model* is the union of all subjective models, or the view from everywhere and everywhen.

Characteristics of objects like beauty and ugliness are present in subjective models but are not present in the objective model because the same object may be viewed as beautiful or ugly by different people. However, that does not necessarily entail that beauty and ugliness do not exist within reality. Thus it is important to explore which aspects of our experience derive from our self and which aspects derive from the world, as well as when that distinction represents a false dichotomy.

2.2 Subjective/Objective Models

The subjective and objective perspectives can be distinguished by asking, "What is different for each of us?" and "What is the same for each of us?" If you see what I see when you stand where I am standing, then what we see is likely to be an objective truth about the world; otherwise, it is probably only a subjective truth. For example, space is typically considered *relative* since every observer has their own location in space ("here"), while time is typically considered *objective* since all observers share a present moment ("now"). However, time is relative according to modern physics, which indicates that our mental models have not caught up with our scientific models.

The divergence of subjective and objective truth allows us to make consistent truth statements about reality by distinguishing truths that are intersubjectively shared from those that are not. Unfortunately, it also strongly reinforces the subject/object dichotomy by supporting the idea that various aspects of our experience exist only within us and not in the world. However, subjective truths may exist as facts of the world; the beauty of a flower may be an aspect of reality in virtue of its context within a multidimensional world.

Although people don't agree about *what* is beautiful, we might wonder if there is consensus about *where* beauty occurs. If we ask neuroscientists, they would probably tell us that the objective location of beauty is in the brain. But from the subjective perspective, things are beautiful *in the world*: happily, we do not fall in love with our brains when we see beauty. But how do we reconcile these multiple perspectives about what beauty is and even where beauty exists? Neither the Objective Model nor any particular Subjective Model can tell the entire story, since doing so requires holding multiple differing points of view.

2.3 Combining Models

Subjectivity occupies a single extended spatiotemporal position, the here-and-now (although that location should be considered as a volume rather than a point in space and time). Objectivity exists everywhere-and-now, although it lacks various subjective qualities such as beauty. Unfortunately, the combination of these two perspectives can lead us to feel like isolated emotional animals in a mechanistic world. However, not all models strongly reify the subjective/objective dichotomy. In particular, the Physical Model does not reinforce this division since it is a larger whole composed of multiple subjective and objective models.

Taking the union of multiple models sometimes leads to seemingly paradoxical features: for example, while coffee tastes *either* good or bad in a Subjective Model, and it tastes *neither* good nor bad in the Objective Model, coffee tastes *both* good and bad in the Physical Model. Thus, while a cup of coffee in the Objective Model is an intersection of experience that excludes any good or bad taste, the coffee as represented by the Physical Model is a union of experience that has both good taste and bad taste. To clarify any apparent contradiction, it helps to understand that all relations correspond to events in various spatiotemporal locations. In other words, the good and bad taste of coffee are abstract relations that generalize different events in the world where coffee is tasted, and those discontiguous events do not contradict one another. However, statements about coffee tasting *universally* good or bad certainly overgeneralize those events, even though coffee tastes good and bad in more specific contexts.

Similarly, the beauty of a flower is known by an observer, but that beauty is not present exclusively within them; the events that correspond to the recognition of that flower's beauty have a location in reality, and therefore generalizations of those events also exist in reality. Expressed more simply, beauty is a part of physical space: while it exists in the mind of an observer, it exists there because of events in the world that are known by that observer, such as flowers signifying the end of winter and the beginning of spring. The inclusion of that temporal context makes flowers meaningful and also requires a high-dimensional space; 3-D objective space is not big enough. Thus, flowers are meaningful in the high-dimensional Subjective and Physical Models because they include that context, while that context is stripped away by the (3-D) Objective Model.

3. The Physical Model

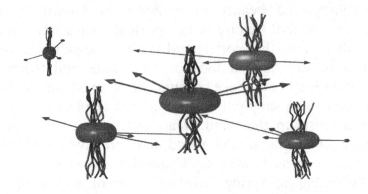

Figure 3: A model of multiple selves.

3.1 *Mind, Emotion, and Body*

Many models analyze the self into a body and a mind. The scientific model further analyzes the body anatomically into several systems and numerous organs and the brain into two hemispheres, four lobes, and several functional units such as the cerebellum. Unfortunately, these anatomical models often do not correspond very well to our subjective experience. For example, they do not provide insight into basic questions like how emotions interact with thoughts.

So how should we analyze the self? There is no single correct answer. The Physical Model developed here combines multiple subjective and objective perspectives, but it is not analyzed into spatially separate subjective and objective components. Rather, it analyzes the self into three overlapping aspects of reality: mental, emotional, and bodily.

The earliest references to body, mind, and bliss as the three aspects of reality occur in various Upanishads as *satchitananda*, a synonym for Brahman. Similar terms are used in Buddhism for the three bodies of a Buddha (as the *trikaya*) and as attributes of God in Abrahamic theology (who is described as all-powerful, all-knowing, and all-good). While not claiming any such lofty parallels with this work, modeling the self and world using these three aspects is beneficial because it accommodates both the body/mind distinction and the emotional aspect of being that is essential to any model of subjective experience.

In this work, these three aspects are defined as follows:

- **Mind** is the *knowing* aspect of a self and is analyzed using references and connections.
- **Emotion** is the *feeling* aspect of a self and is analyzed using energy.
- **Body** is the *being* aspect of a self and is analyzed using parts and wholes.

The Physical Model combines all subjective and objective perspectives just as physical space does, and is analyzed in terms of these three inseparable aspects of reality. This model of reality, since it contains both subjective and objective truths, can be visualized as a mind that can appreciate all subjective points of view. This model is therefore similar to panpsychism, or the belief that everything is conscious. But what is it to be conscious? Without directly answering that question, understanding the self in less subjective terms might involve viewing the body as material, the emotions as energetic, and the mind as connective.

3.2 Kindness

A person's models of self and world often have a direct impact on their degree of kindness. To understand this relation, it is useful to analyze kindness into kindness shown to our self and kindness shown to others.

The kindness shown to our self is affected by models of body and mind in at least two ways. First, the notion of body explored in this work is not limited to the 3-D body, so as we are physically interconnected in many dimensions, individual ethics become more tightly enmeshed with collective ethics. Second, since the location of our mind or awareness is often outside of the body, our mind often has a natural concern for others.

Showing kindness to others, although not necessary, is required if we decide to embody the Physical Model (for more details, see *Chapter 15: Empathy*). While this work strives to avoid moralistic injunctions, hopefully the adoption of the Physical Model is shown to be a desirable option for both our self and others.

Exercise: Asking

Spend some time considering who you are.

What are your body and mind made of?

How is your mind different from your body?

*Are emotions such as love
an essential aspect of your being?*

*Do your mind and body exist in three dimensions?
Do they exist in the same place and time?*

Does your concept of self extend beyond your body?

*Is it possible for a body to be conscious,
or does consciousness require a mind?*

PART II

SPACETIME

Using the metaphor of space as a framework to model all subjective and objective phenomena requires many dimensions, each of which measures an arbitrary objective or subjective characteristic. For example, a 3-D red-green-blue color space on a 2-D piece of paper creates a 5-D space that associates a color with every location on the page. Thus, specifying the location of an object in increasingly higher dimensions allows describing *what* an object is in virtue of *where* that object is.

Notably, the dimensionality of space is shared by the objects within it. For example, a piece of paper has some thickness if it exists in 3-D space, even though it approximates a 2-D object. Since current theories of physics model space as at least 4-D, real objects have four or more dimensions. But before considering what it means for objects to be multidimensional, we first consider several features of spacetime.

4. The Rug Model

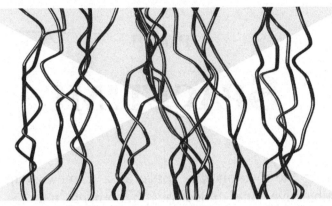

Figure 4: Multiple spatiotemporal strings within a rug.

4.1 *The Metaphor of the Rug*

The Rug Model is a metaphor for the world in which objects correspond to strings arranged lengthwise within a rug. Each string is extended through time, so an object at a single moment corresponds to the cross section of a string. In some areas of the rug the strings are tightly bound by each other, while in other areas the rug is loosely knit. No string is entirely free: each is interwoven with other strings, and pulling on any string affects all of the strings with which it is connected.

Our material body is like a string within this rug; our present actions affect both the past and future, and actions in the past and future affect the present. We have some freedom to move about, although we are partially constrained by other strings. Our birth and death correspond to the beginning and end of a string, and throughout its length we are connected by local strings to more remote strings.

4.2 Action on a String

Since the Rug Model uses the analogy of a completed rug which can be changed at any location, it portrays both the past and future as partially free and partially fixed. The Rug Model is thus radically different from the more common view that the future is free and the past is fixed. Neither of these views can be proven, since we cannot visit the past or future for verification. Similarly, the hypothesis that causality is unidirectional as opposed to bidirectional cannot be confirmed. That said, it makes sense to select the simpler of these alternatives unless there are good reasons to introduce additional complexity.[3]

Unfortunately, language makes it difficult to talk about alternate views of time. It is not possible for the past or the future to *exist* within the syntax of English: we can only say that the past "existed" or that the future "will exist". For that reason, the Rug Model is useful for visualizing both forward and backward causality as it allows us to transcend the view that the present is the only time that can change or have causal impact.

4.3 Presentism and Eternalism

The Block Universe Model is a view of reality in which the past and the future are both fixed. Within this (eternalist) model, each of us experiences a relative here-and-now that is not the same for anyone else. The "block" refers to a hypercube that usually corresponds to a 4-D block comprising 3-D space and 1-D time, but it can represent arbitrarily high dimensions, and it corresponds to spacetime diagrams when limited to 1-D space and 1-D time.

The Growing Block Universe Model is a view of reality in which the past is fixed and the future is free. This (presentist) model is a version of the Block Universe Model that is being completed: the future does not "exist" and events are added to the block as time progresses. In this model, reality is being created rather than being discovered.

Both block models identify the presence of the block with being fixed or determined. In contrast, the Rug Model envisions a completed rug that can undergo change at any location, and in which causality operates in both temporal directions. Thus, worldlines in the Rug Model are not fixed by their presence or absence as in the block views, but by their interconnection with other worldlines.

5. Measuring Space

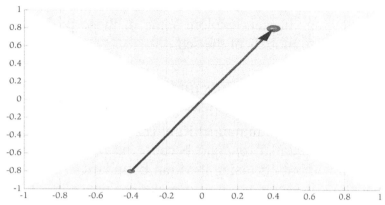

Figure 5: A constant velocity vector in spacetime.

5.1 *The Spacetime Model*

It is not generally necessary to understand the theoretical details of spacetime or geometry, but they can help to recognize outdated or incorrect models in our language and thought. Therefore, this chapter briefly discusses two important aspects of the geometry of space: dimensionality and continuity.

Different geometries describe space in different ways, so the choice of geometry partially determines our world-model. For example, the notion that only the present exists or that time flows forward are aspects of a geometry that is embedded in both our understanding and in the syntax of the language that we use. In particular, English and other languages implicitly describe events in the world as a collection of 3-D things (represented by noun phrases) that undergo change in the fourth dimension (represented by verb phrases).

If we do not understand language as a low-dimensional model of a high-dimensional world, then we are prone to mistakenly reify language and see 3-D things as "real" objects in the (multidimensional) world. Unfortunately, that mistake is associated with a host of problems, as it entails that objects exist independently of time, either instantaneously or in virtue of some permanent essence. The following chapters explore some of those problems as they pertain to models of the self.

5.2 Points and Instants

Continuity entails that there are no smallest (or integral) parts. As stated by Immanuel Kant (1781, Ch2, 3.2), "Space and time are *quanta continua* because no part of them can be given, without enclosing it within boundaries (points and moments)". It seems natural to make the related claim that the nature of space is continuous and that discontinuity or discreteness is created by generalizations of *sameness* by the conceptual mind.

Albert Einstein was a staunch defender of continuity within theoretical physics, although many physicists believe that reality is quantized (in the sense of quantum physics).[4] In mathematics, continuous and discrete entities are typically unified using the theory of point-sets and the concept of (actual) infinity. However, using a model in which points *constitute* space is probably not the best choice for either physical or conceptual spaces, so this work uses point-free topology as its geometry (for more detailed justification, see Rogers, 2020).

Using point-free topology as a model of spacetime entails that space and time are treated in a similar manner. Thus, just as space does not consist of points, time does not consist of instants: instead, all parts of spacetime are multidimensional events or spatiotemporal regions. Perhaps one day, our language will reflect this model by treating the present like a relative and specious moment rather than a shared objective instant.

5.3 Thompson's Lamp

Thompson's Lamp is a paradox that can be used to argue for point-free geometries as models of the world by demonstrating the inconsistency of an infinite set of instants. To understand the paradox, imagine that we repeatedly flip the switch of a lamp over the course of one minute. We flip the switch at the beginning of the minute and flip it again after 1/2 minute. We flip it when there is 1/4 minute left, 1/8th minute left, 1/16th minute left, etc., in an inverse geometrical progression that involves flipping the switch "an infinite" number of times by the time the minute is over.[5]

The paradox becomes evident by asking if the lamp is on or off at the end of the minute. According to point-set mathematics, this non-converging series of switch-flipping does not have a final value, which is problematic because in reality, the lamp is going to be either on or off. Happily, the creation of this theoretically impossible scenario is prevented by using point-free topology as a model.[6]

5.4 Parts and Wholes

Point-free topologies combine continuous and discrete spaces by using boundaries. In psychological terms, nominal boundaries between continuous regions are imputed by concepts. To use a line as an example, zero-dimensional points can create boundaries within a line, but they cannot *constitute* that line because they do not occupy any space along its length. More concretely, cutting a loaf of bread in half with a knife produces left and right halves, but it does not produce an infinitely small slice of bread corresponding to the knife edge. Rather, the knife merely divides the bread (which is how points divide lines within point-free topologies).

Extending this reasoning to higher dimensions, all objects occupy regions of continuous physical space that are separated from each other by conceptual boundaries.[7]

One advantage of this approach is the elimination of several topological paradoxes related to open and closed shapes that arise from using point-sets (see Rogers, 2020). Another advantage is that mental boundaries can distinguish one thing from another without being confused with the things they divide (since they do not substantially exist within that space).

6. Worldlines

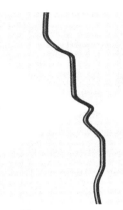

Figure 6: A worldline.

6.1 *Beyond Spacetime*

Modern theories of physics routinely use four or more dimensions, but unfortunately the visualization of that many dimensions at one time is difficult if not impossible. However, space and time can be plotted on a graph called a spacetime diagram by reducing 3-D space to a 1-D approximation (see *Appendix A: Spacetime Diagrams*). Objects are represented in spacetime diagrams by trajectories through space and time called *worldlines*.

Using multiple worldlines allows multiple objects to be represented, but multiple worldlines can also represent the existence of a single object in multiple alternate realities. Thus, by depicting the different possible states of an object as different worldlines, spacetime diagrams can represent a fifth dimension: possibility.

6.2 *Determinism and Freedom*

The behavior of large-scale objects is often believed to be *deterministic*, meaning that there are laws of nature that objects are required to follow. If everything in the world is deterministic, then knowing the laws of nature and the current state of affairs makes it possible to predict the future. As an inalterable future seems not to allow sufficient freedom for personal responsibility, randomness or probability are sometimes introduced to counteract the extreme inalterability of determinism.

The theory of *free will*, on the other hand, asserts that humans and possibly other objects are free. If everything is free, then nothing is determined and even tiny particles choose what to do. In that case, it would be logical to build bridges between domain-specific areas of language, such as by expressing the law of gravitation in terms of the will of all things to gravitate toward one another. On the other hand, if only humans are free, then building such a bridge would create confusion. If both free will and deterministic laws of nature are present in the world, then we need to understand how they can peacefully coexist.

6.3 *Is Will the Determinism Within Us?*

It is tenuous for freedom and determinism to exist side by side, since free causes are not the same as deterministic causes. But if the material of the universe follows deterministic laws, and the mind directs what its material body does, then what is the relation between these two seemingly redundant sources of action?

One way to reconcile these two sources is to recast free will as the determination of the individual. The determinism that derives from inside the individual is the will of that individual, or what that individual chooses to do. This is related to Arthur Schopenhauer's claim that we are free to choose to do what we will, but we are not free to choose that will, implying that there isn't an infinite regress with respect to our freedom. The position taken here is that a person or any other object is free or self-determined to the extent that they are not determined by other objects, and in keeping with the Rug Model, objects are determined by both past and future interactions. In one sense this is trivially true: things are free unless they are not. However, it can be seen as similar to Edwin Schrödinger's theory of wave function collapse, a conjecture that objects can exist in different states at the same time until the system is observed or it interacts with some other system.

7. Causality

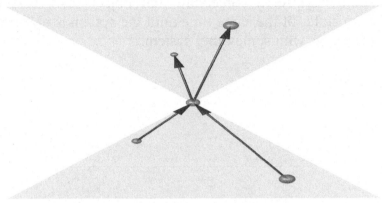

Figure 7: Causally connected events.

7.1 *The Billiards Model*

The Billiards Model illustrates a view of causation that is both popular and problematic. Imagine a shot where a player hits the cue ball, which caroms off the two ball and knocks into the eight. This series of events can be visualized as an interaction beginning with a single cause (the cue stick) that involves two collisions between three different balls. This description connotes that all events have a single cause and that events can only affect subsequent events.

Single-cause models of causation have several advantages over multiple-cause models. One advantage is that single causes are relatively easy to understand and reason with: if a significant event occurs, it is easier to find a single responsible cause. Another is that seeing our self as the single sufficient cause for some effect has survival value. For example, while there can be serious consequences for missing the opportunity to control significant outcomes, committing an over-attribution error by erroneously believing that we are responsible for a spurious effect typically results only in superstitious behavior. Thus, the benefit of correctly recognizing our responsibility for an event is greater than the cost of trying to control uncontrollable events.

7.2 Causality and Time

Temporally reversing the sequence of interactions in the billiards example given previously takes three people with cue sticks, each of whom has to hit a ball at its terminal position to drive it back to the point of impact, coordinating with the other shooters to move the cue ball back to its original position.[8] Compared to the forward trajectory of the cue ball, the reverse trajectory requires a magnificently complex coordination of events.

However, inverting the cue ball's trajectory does not change the direction of causality: the cue ball moves through a trajectory and then reverses that trajectory, all of which occurs in the same temporal direction. The cue ball is back where it started, but at a later point in time; it returns to the "same" point in time only if time is treated as a measure of change. If time is treated as a dimension of reality, these actions remain causal rather than retrocausal. Still, this visualization is useful to understand retrocausality.

The single-cause model of the world may itself be partially responsible for the belief that causality is not invertible, since it makes backward causation relatively more difficult. A more relativistic model would treat every one of the billiard balls as a cause. Although that makes the interaction diagram going forward a complex set of contributing causes, it also makes going backward relatively less complicated.[9]

7.3 *Causality and Scale*

Another feature of the common causal model is the implicit bias that small-scale changes determine large-scale changes. Presumably, that reductionistic bias is due to knowing things through analysis more often than synthesis, or knowing an object's parts better than its wholes. While a reductionistic approach partially works for mechanisms with internal sources of action, it is less useful for explaining the actions of billiard balls in terms of the parts of those balls. But if causality occurs only *through* time, then it is impossible for small-scale changes to simultaneously cause large-scale changes or vice versa.

If causality allowed one event to simultaneously affect another at some spatiotemporal distance, then it would at least be possible for small-scale changes to cause large-scale changes. But when small-scale phenomena and large-scale phenomena overlap, it is sometimes equally valid (or invalid) to say that the movement of molecules determines our behavior as it is to say that behavioral forces determine the movement of our molecules.

8. Retrocausality

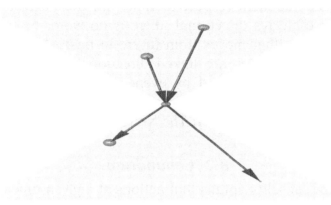

Figure 8: Retrocausally connected events.

8.1 *Is Time Bidirectional?*

In this work, time is assumed to be a bidirectional dimension, as are the spatial dimensions. Therefore, even though it is impossible to prove that either the past or the future can be changed, it is important to explore adding retrocausality (or reverse-causation) to the standard causal model since it may counteract several limiting beliefs that we hold unnecessarily.[10]

There are two significantly different approaches to investigating the possibility of temporal symmetry. One approach is based on the observation that some processes are not reversible, such as ripples on a lake that spread exclusively outwards from a point of impact. Although there are physical sinks in addition to physical sources, each type of process aligns with a particular temporal direction (for a more thorough investigation, see Price, 1996). Thus, while certain events have an orientation in time, physics does not support the notion that *time itself* flows in only one direction.

A more psychological approach to thinking about the directionality of time examines why we experience time so differently from the three spatial dimensions. In fact, there are several ways in which our cognitive processes are unidirectional with respect to time. On the linguistic side, verbs are always directional: there is no word for engaging in an action that moves from future to past. On the neural side, our memories are linked directionally: we remember that event X is followed by event Y much better than we remember that event Y is preceded by event X (this subject is revisited in *Section 11.4: The Nervous System Model*).

8.2 Conundrums

Retrocausality entails that actions at a given time change events at a previous time. One way this might work is by altering particles that travel backwards in time. Another way is to simply change our understanding by stipulating that all causal processes are also retrocausal. In other words, effects necessitate their causes just as causes necessitate their effects. For example, just as the prior motion of the cue *causes* the object ball to move when they collide, the subsequent movement of the object ball *retrocauses* the cue ball to hit it: one pulls the probability of occurrence just as the other pushes it.

Both forward causality and retrocausality can be explained in terms of the connected worldlines of causally linked objects. However, encountering the notion of retrocausality for the first time often raises several questions:[11]

How are we not colliding with objects from the past and future if they exist? The Rug Model encourages us to see the past and future as *similar to* the present in that both the past and future have causal efficacy, but that does not mean that the past and future are *in* the present. Thus, the worldlines of objects can affect each other if they are connected with one another, regardless of whether that connection is in the past, present, or future.

If we exist throughout time, why does sensation happen only in the present? The Rug Model supports the claim that our bodies "exist" throughout some temporal interval, rather than only at a present instant. But if we are spatiotemporal volumes that exist from some time in the past until some time in the future, then why do our senses sense only the here-and-now? Well, that's just what subjectivity is: we *are* located in space and time, and while our senses process temporally narrow events in the here-and-now, our material body is temporally extended beyond the here-and-now. In other words, sensory events take place on a much smaller time scale than the span of the body that contains those sensory events.

Why does time appear to flow in only one direction? Language may describe change in only one direction, but that does not imply that time itself has a direction. While there are processes such as entropy that always flow in the same direction and in accord with the structure of our memories, it is not justified to abstract a moving, objective phenomenon called time from multiple subjective processes. Rather, some processes align in the temporal direction just as gravity often causes objects to move in the same spatial direction.[12]

8.3 Entanglement

There are extraordinary experiments in quantum physics that demonstrate *entanglement*, wherein spatially separated objects become causally linked with one another. The relation between entangled objects can be understood in several ways. One theory is that entangled objects form a single discontiguous object. Another theory is that causality operates instantaneously between entangled particles, a phenomenon that Albert Einstein called "spooky actions at a distance". The theory proposed here is that the action of both entanglement and *karma* depends on retrocausality.[13]

In more detail, the instantaneous effects between karmically connected objects can be explained by allowing a causal chain that propagates retrocausally into the past, where one particle changes the other and that change propagates causally back to the present. This process can create instantaneous effects because it occurs *within* time. According to this understanding, causation travels both backwards and forwards along the worldlines of objects. Since causality flows through time, things can be causally local that are not spatially local and therefore causes can have instantaneous effects at a distance. Stated equivalently using the Rug Model, we might pull on a string and cause a change to a parallel thread, but that change only constitutes non-local action with respect to a cross-section of that rug.

8.4 *Temporal Consistency*

Many stories about time travel involve a paradoxical inconsistency that is produced by a single worldline revisiting the same spacetime. Retrocausality also invites this potential for inconsistency: our memories may be inconsistent with respect to a changed past unless changes to the past immediately propagate to the present such that our memory of previous events is instantly changed.

Most models assume that reality must be consistent, or that it may be probabilistic but that it cannot be paradoxical. Accordingly, one way to handle inconsistency is to treat it as probabilistic consistency. In other words, inconsistency in spacetime can be accommodated by using the dimension of possibility. To ensure that the past and future are probabilistically consistent with those changes, changes to the present are immediately propagated backward and forward. Since our memories must also be consistent with the world, this indicates that our mental images have a resonant relationship with the events that they reference in the world.

Exercise: Visualizing

Visualize things in space.

Your visualization should be clearly defined.

It may help to empathize with the visualized objects,
or to visualize familiar objects.

Attempt to visualize events in both space and time.

If you cannot imagine even simple objects,
take your environment as a support:
visualize what you see,
and continue that visualization with closed eyes.

PART III

MIND

Although we all *have* minds, or perhaps *are* minds, many of us are only vaguely aware of what a mind is. We know that mind is a thinking thing, but sometimes forget that thoughts are abstract and that the way they become abstract is by forgetting numerous particular details. We know that the mind is not the body, but where to draw the line between mind and body has historically been a subject of much debate.

Although it somewhat oversimplifies things, this work categorizes a thing as a mind if and only if it references something else. In contrast, bodies are non-referential.

9. Conceptual Spaces

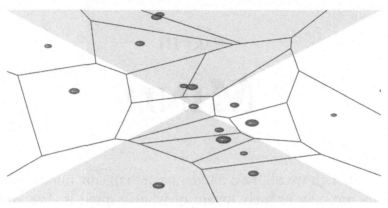

Figure 9: Conceptual regions.

9.1 *Conceptual Space*

Concepts are references that exist both in the space of the objects that they reference and in a conceptual space. The relations between concepts in conceptual space reflect the relations between their associated objects in physical space; this arrangement is called an *isomorphism*. For example, the color orange has a wavelength between the red and yellow wavelengths, so in conceptual space, the concept of orange is situated between the concepts of red and yellow. As a result of this isomorphism, any concept can represent any object: the orange concept and the orange object are not required to be physically similar.

The relativity of concepts can be understood by modeling them as boundaries, since boundaries structure a space but do not exist in that space (this is depicted in Figure 9). Visually, this is similar to viewing reality through a stained-glass window, where the frames between the window panes correspond to concepts, and the granularity of the panes determines the precision with which reality is conceptualized.[14]

9.2 Properties of Concepts

Concepts and conceptual spaces have several properties that influence how the world is known:

- Concepts are known relative to one another, rather than essentially.
- Concepts are discrete, although they may refer to continuous regions or other concepts.
- Conceptual spaces and the spaces to which they refer may have differing dimensionality.

Although these features are generally beneficial, they may cause the misinterpretation of reality. For example, understanding the world in terms of concepts might lead us to believe that the physical objects themselves are entirely relative, discrete, or 3-D. These mistakes violate the dictum of Alfred Korzybski: the map is not the territory.

The confusion of the map with the territory is especially significant because our model of reality often guides our emotional attachment, as when our enjoyment of objects causes us to become attached to the concepts by which we know those objects. One problematic feature of such attachment is that concepts are typically more permanent than the objects to which they refer, which results in continued suffering when those objects eventually disintegrate.

9.3 Relative and Absolute

When we talk about an orange object, our words categorize it and distinguish it from other objects, but they don't convey or say anything about the object directly. However, such conceptual relativity is probably not the whole story about how we know the world: if it were, we would know the world only metaphorically. Since the categorization of an object seems to depend on the object itself, philosophical systems sometimes posit that objects have an absolute and directly known aspect in addition to their relative and conceptual aspect; for example, see Thackchoe (2011).

If we experience the absolute aspect of objects independent of our categorization of them, then we know qualities of objects that are impossible to express. However, we can still express *how* we know those qualities, such as being in some way directly connected with those objects. Also, even knowing that there is something inexpressible of which we can be aware helps our quest for self-knowledge, or rather, our quest for self-feeling.

10. Connectionism

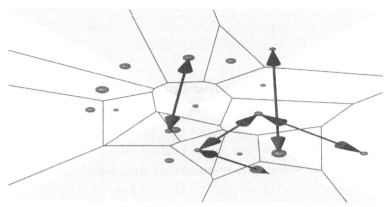

Figure 10: Connections between conceptual regions.

10.1 *The Connectionist Model*

Connectionism generally refers to a collection of neural architectures that are used to model the brain. It derives from an Aristotelian philosophy called associationism, according to which the mind is composed of mutually associated concepts. The mental association between any two concepts has a degree or strength that is determined by the karma or association between their corresponding objects.

The Connectionist Model explains several subconscious phenomena, and as such it facilitates being aware of mental operations that are difficult to observe. For example, connectionism can be used to illustrate *priming*, a phenomenon where all concepts associated with the active concept become primed. Priming does not necessarily entail the activation or awareness of a concept, although primed concepts are more likely to subsequently arise explicitly as thoughts.

As a concrete example of how mental connections guide behavior, suppose we love coffee and we enter a room where there is a sweet little americano on the table. The strong positive connection will probably pull our attention, which temporarily *activates* the coffee-concept and obfuscates other concepts. That differential activation within the network of concepts guides our subsequent thought and behavior.

10.2 *Subjective Connectionism*

The Connectionist Model can be used as a model of our lived subjective experience by projecting our mental connections onto the world and understanding our experience of the world in terms of that subjective overlay. To do so, visualize being at the center of a network of threads that connects us with every object in the world that we see, hear, smell, taste, or touch. The thickness of each thread corresponds to the strength of that connection, and objects that don't have any threads tied to them go unnoticed. Areas of the world that we love or hate are better represented, as are strongly sensed areas such as our fingertips.

The concepts in the network become active as we encounter their referent objects in the world, and the effect of that activity is *knowing* those objects, although discursive thought about those objects may not arise. Activated concepts also prime one another in virtue of our experience of the connection between them. To the degree that the activated concepts are liked or disliked, they draw us toward or push us away from their corresponding objects.

10.3 *Modeling Equanimity*

One way that the Connectionist Model can help us is to facilitate becoming more equanimous, which it does by providing a platform upon which to define equanimity. For example, we might represent equanimity as resting at the center of a sphere of objects, where the visualized strings tying us to those objects are neither too tight nor too loose.

Defining equanimity in terms of balanced connections illustrates that we need good conceptual representations of many different objects. For example, we cannot find the center of a room if we see only two walls, a floor, and a ceiling. As the number of conceptual representations of the room increases, our ability to find equilibrium at the center improves. An accurate representation of the room also requires that we are not strongly attracted to or repulsed by its contents; if the smell of coffee pulls our attention too strongly, equanimity is lost and we fail to remain centered.

Thus, the Connectionist Model facilitates developing the meta-awareness that allows us to observe our equanimity or lack thereof, and may ultimately help us to refine or become more in touch with our feeling of equanimity.

11. What is the Mind?

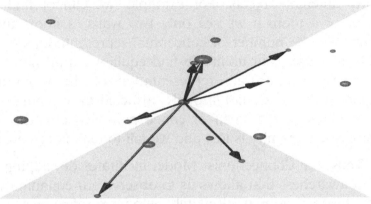

Figure 11: Mental references to various events.

11.1 *Mind is Referential*

Our mind is referential. It is composed of references from the brain to referenced objects, so it has a location that covers both subject and object.

- From the subjective perspective, the mind is equivalent to its referential content, or objects that are perceived *in the world.*
- From the objective perspective, the mind is a set of references *in the brain,* or a set of neurons whose referential content is not perceived.

Each mental reference is analogous to a neuron with the same dualistic property: we can look *at* the neuron from the objective point of view (and see a part of the subject), or we can look *through* the neuron from the subjective point of view (and see a part of the object referenced by that neuron). In other words, we subjectively perceive distant objects rather than the things in our brain that enable us to see those objects. This distinction is usually beneficial: it would be problematic if we perceived our neurons as large dendritic cells floating in space.

11.2 Minds Exist at Different Scales

Minds exist at different scales or levels of organization. For example, just as our brains are minds, the world is a mind (at least in the sense that it is referential, and perhaps in the sense that it is conscious).

The speculation that the world is aware may seem odd because if the world had a mind, we would presumably know it and possibly talk to it. But if neurons could talk, and we asked one if it was a part of a brain, it might answer, "What are you talking about? I'm just here eating intracellular soup, listening to my nervous neighbors yelling, and often yelling back." As a general rule, the collective wisdom of a mind does not exist in any one of its references.

Similarly, the world's wisdom is probably not embodied in any one of us, so our ignorance of a larger world-mind is not good evidence that one does not exist. In fact, the neural analogy suggests that a world-mind *does* exist because intelligence seems to increase at higher levels of organization. The further hypothesis that the world is a mind that has subjective experience, however, depends on our theory of consciousness. For example, the world is not a mind if consciousness is a byproduct of the brain, while it is a mind if consciousness is simply what it feels like to be material.[15]

11.3 Minds Exist at Different Levels

The conceptual references that constitute a mind may reference a body or other references. Arranging those references such that information flows in the same direction creates a conceptual hierarchy which consists of *referential levels*, where each level is a map of the previous level. All information is supplied at the initial or bodily level, and subsequent mental levels illuminate different truths about that information. The non-referential or bodily level is also called the ground, since it acts as a substrate for all subsequent referential levels.

If the existence of an object as a non-referential ground is determined by our point of view, then perhaps everything is referential from some point of view. In other words, if the determination of things as referential depends on our point of view, then there is no ultimate ground from all perspectives.[16] One of the earliest occurrences of this no-ground hypothesis occurs implicitly in a Hindu metaphor for reality called the *Net of Indra*, which models reality as a net of jewels in which each jewel reflects all of the others.

11.4 *The Nervous System Model*

The Nervous System Model maps referential levels onto the nervous system by treating neurons as references. Sensory neurons constitute the lowest referential level and sense the body, while interneurons at higher levels reference those references. The Nervous System Model is significantly more comprehensible than actual nervous systems, which often have a recurrent structure and are terrifically more complex.

One fascinating characteristic of the spatial representation of the Nervous System Model is that it is *not* 4-D: events are bidirectionally connected in the three spatial dimensions while they are connected only forwards in the temporal dimension. This is probably related to the fact that the hippocampus, an organ of the brain responsible for spatial representation, is limited to three dimensions (the representation of temporally complex events can only be achieved by relying on other brain areas). As a practical example, the concepts corresponding to the letters of the alphabet are usually linked to one another in this way, so that iterating over those letters in forward order is trivial while reverse iteration is more difficult.

The Nervous System Model can be viewed as a type of Map and Vehicle Model in which the network of references is a map that is traversed by awareness. Although the nervous system corresponds to the map, it is not clear what physiologically corresponds to the vehicle that enables awareness of the map. One possibility is that material is inherently conscious. That does not mean that arbitrary matter is capable of thought or complex emotions, but rather that it feels like something to exist, independent of a mind and the subject/object structure that mental references create. However, the inherent consciousness of the body may become subject/object awareness if that body contains references (i.e., if it is a mind).

12. Where is the Mind?

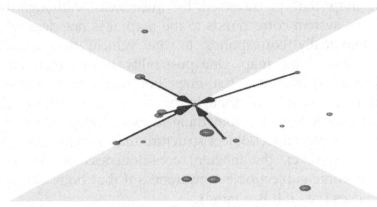

Figure 12: Mind as the effect of referenced events.

12.1 *Where is the Mind?*

Since the mind is referential, the mind viewed subjectively and the mind viewed objectively have different locations: the brain is in the subject and the mind (or the location of mental awareness) is in the object. Colloquially, we might paraphrase this duality as, "The mind is not the brain".[17] To illustrate the potential confusion between the subjective and objective points of view, consider the following statements:

- We are a mind within a body.
- We are a body within a mind.

The first statement takes the objective perspective, which models human minds as things within the bodies of humans, as do physiology texts. Thus, the mind is objectively located where neurons are located (i.e., throughout the body, although predominantly in the brain and spinal cord). So from the objective perspective, the body is larger than the mind.

The second statement takes the subjective perspective, according to which the experience of our bodies occurs within our minds. Thus, the mind is subjectively located wherever our awareness is directed. If our awareness remained within our body, then we would know nothing but our body. So from the subjective perspective, the mind is larger than the body.[18]

Neither of these two somewhat contradictory statements is invalid, although the subjective perspective receives relatively little attention because the objective perspective is more heavily reinforced by the scientific method. Although the objective and subjective points of view may not be able to be entirely reconciled, it may help to distinguish how the terms "mind" and "body" are used. For example, we might experience a sensation-body or concept body, within a mind (or nervous system), within a physical-body. In that case, there may be confusion between the concept-body that results from our understanding and the physical-body that represents how reality actually is. However, this entails adopting the view from the outside looking in, and entails prioritizing the objective or material view. It may be equally correct to stipulate that we are a physical-mind, within a body, within a conceptual-mind, which represents the view from the inside looking out, and entails prioritizing the subjective or mental view.

12.2 *Subject and Object*

While mental representations exist in the subject, they are often the effects of objects. For example, the visual image of a chair is a result of that chair: in other words, that chair is a necessary cause. So are mental representations the result of the brain, or are they the result of the represented object?[19] In English, we *see* objects but we *have* ideas, which suggests that perceptions are the result of what is perceived while ideas are the result of the mind. If our ideas are caused by our perceptions, however, then to what degree do we think thoughts and to what degree do thoughts think us?

Although this question represents somewhat of a false dichotomy, it highlights two different notions of identity. The bodily or material perspective defines identity in terms of material containment, while the mental or referential perspective defines identity in terms of references. We might summarize these views of identity by saying that a part belongs to its whole while a reference belongs to its referent, much as an effect belongs to its cause.[20] Referential identity is thus non-materialistic because it entails that the identity of a thing does not exist entirely where that thing materially exists. Consider whether a reflection is a result of the reflected object or the mirror that reflects that object. It is difficult to argue that mirrors are responsible for their reflections if they do not choose what they reflect. Further, not only are mirrors unable to choose their content, but they cannot even decide to reflect or not, just as an untrained mind cannot choose to think or not.

12.3 *Mind is Everywhere*

Linguistically, the subjective or first-person location is almost entirely synonymous with the body's location rather than the location of awareness. While we extend our mental and emotional identity in acts of creation and empathy, physical location remains paramount when determining the location at which we exist. If we identify with the location of our awareness, on the other hand, how might we behave differently?[21]

If we envision ourselves as contiguous objects that *bring the outside world in* by seeing and hearing, our materialistic subjective locus will not substantially shift. However, to the degree that we identify with the contents of our perception, we are everywhere that we perceive, and to the degree that we identify with the content of our concepts, we are everywhere that we think about. So while we are partially the material body and brain which is *here*, we are also partially a mind which is constituted by events that are *there.* Since by definition we cannot perceive or conceive beyond those mental limits, we might say that from the subjective point of view, the mind is everywhere and everywhen.

Exercise: Knowing

Analyze your experience,
keeping your mind at a particular epistemic level.[22]

For example, you might perceive a book,
or you might know that it is a book,
or you might think, "Oh, a book!".

Be aware only of thought:
think about things.

Be aware only of knowing:
know without thinking.

Be aware only of perception:
perceive without thinking or knowing.

Be aware only of being:
see if there is an awareness of simply being,
without thinking, knowing, or perceiving.

PART IV

EMOTION

Models of emotion are relatively sparse compared to the wide variety of models of mind and body. This may be partially responsible for the lack of agreement about the number of emotions or how they are related to mind and body. Emotions have historically been seen as forces that oppose the rational operation of mind, and therefore they are often repressed. In modern culture, we increasingly recognize the importance of emotional intelligence, but we don't agree on suitable models for its development. We advocate for love, but have trouble saying what love is.

To make emotions easier to model, this work relies on the analogy between emotion and energy. Specifically, emotion is understood as the energetic aspect of being, which propels the movement of our minds and bodies. To keep things simple, emotions are divided into four categories corresponding to either potential energy, two simple kinetic energies that attract and repel, or the class of all other energies that tend to be more complex as a result of being tied to multiple concepts.

13. Types of Emotions

Figure 13: Emotional energy.

13.1 *Potential Emotion*

If energy is analogous to emotion, then potential energy is analogous to the ability to feel. Potential emotion is emotion that has not kinetically manifested, and can also be called emotional capacity. The relation between potential and kinetic emotion is similar to wisdom that has not manifested into a particular thought, just as the absence of emotion is similar to ignorance.

Many people assert that it feels like something to merely exist, in which case potential emotion might be called love (*agape*), bliss (*ananda*), buddha nature (*tathāgatagarbha*), or more colloquially, heart.

13.2 *Attraction and Aversion*

Attraction and aversion are perhaps the two most basic emotions, which often evolve into various flavors of love and hate. Energetically they correspond to gravitating toward and pushing away from the objects for which they are felt, although that proximity or distance should be understood more generally than a relation in 3-D space. For example, we might desire to be similar to the object for which an emotion is felt rather than physically close to it.

Although attraction and aversion are directed forces, they are not antithetical to equanimity as long as they are balanced by other energies (i.e., equanimity does not require the absence of energy). Because the energy underlying emotions is essential to our well-being, the difference between having emotional potential and being emotionless is critical. Thus, while feeling attraction to a beautiful object is unbalanced by itself, equanimity can be maintained by simultaneously feeling unattracted from a different perspective.

13.3 *Complex Emotions*

Emotions become more complex in proportion to the number of concepts with which they are connected. For example, the interaction between attraction/aversion and the conceptual self/other dichotomy may create attraction to self and aversion to other (or pride), or aversion to self and attraction to other (or jealousy). Although complex emotions make equanimity increasingly difficult to maintain, the prolific differentiation of emotional energies eventually leads to greater intuitive wisdom.

Subjectively, emotions are experienced in both the body and the location of their object (i.e., in the location of the referent of the concept to which the emotion is tied). For example, if we regard someone as beautiful, the location of that subjectively experienced beauty is felt both in our bodies and in the world at the position of the beautiful object. While that feeling is typically regarded as a subjective sensation, it may also feel like something to be loved; for a related discussion about the bidirectionally of knowing, see *Section 16.4: The Witness Model*.

Precisely identifying the location of various emotions is often difficult because of their tremendous complexity; they are not defined by a relatively small number of boundaries, as are individual concepts. In fact, emotions frequently have a compound location due to their parallel operation. So while simple emotions such as anger and lust are often associated with the head and groin, the location of most emotions is considerably more complex.

13.4 *Emotions as Properties*

The suggestion that emotions exist in the world, even from a subjective point of view, may be objectionable to people who see the world as composed of particles rather than properties. In this work, the duality between particles and properties exists in the continuum that ranges from space to mind (in which things are specific and generic, respectively). Thus, specific things are defined by *where* they are and generic things are defined by *what* they are.[23]

While the distinction between particles and properties is quite useful, it is often unnecessarily conflated with the distinction between self and world. Materialistic philosophy contends that the world (without the life forms within it) consists exclusively of specific objects, while minds perceive and categorize those specific objects to create generalized concepts. Thus, materialism often views the world as *meaningless* because it has no inherent generalizations. However, objects in the world may be described as intersections of properties rather than as unions of particles, as occurs in more idealistic philosophies such as Platonism, and those properties are more often meaningful. So while it may be anthropomorphic to say that human emotions exist in a world without humans, it may be valid to describe reality as both beautiful and ugly in virtue of different events in the world. For example, beauty is a property which may correctly generalize a number of events in which flowers are appreciated by humming birds in spring. While that property of beauty is not a material part of the flower, it is a material *whole* of that flower and those birds. Thus, those flowers have the condition of being beautiful for some subjective definition of beauty even if that beauty is not always appreciated by an observer. Presumably, the Objective Model of the flower leads to that flower mistakenly being identified exclusively with its parts, since the intrinsic parts of a flower are seen as "more permanent" than its extrinsic wholes.

14. Emotional Energy

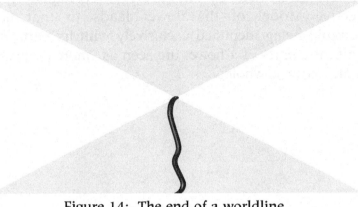

Figure 14: The end of a worldline.

14.1 *Toxic Emotions*

Emotions such as love or anger can be regarded as good or bad things. Love is often considered a good thing, but it may devolve into unhealthy forms of dependence. Anger is often considered a bad thing, but perhaps it is justified when sudden action prevents greater harm.

To clarify this ambiguity, emotions that are always detrimental are called *toxic emotions*. Toxic emotions are negative states that result from confused thoughts or an incomplete understanding in combination with some underlying energy. Although that confusion needs to be clarified if we wish to become emotionally healthy, the underlying energy is beneficial and should not be eliminated. As that confusion acts to obscure or poison the underlying energy, it is called an obscuration. Obscurations may also be called klehsas, sins, or more colloquially, our "issues".

14.2 *Emotional Purification*

In order to cultivate equanimity, it is necessary to purify our emotions. In spiritual contexts, we wish to know how to eliminate our obscurations, wash our sins, or get clear. In therapeutic contexts, we wish to know how to uncover repressed emotions or expose the shadow so that psychoanalysis becomes possible.

Uncomplicated suggestions for purification such as *relax*, *pray*, *love*, or *meditate* may be sufficient to counteract whatever ignorance or disease may be present, especially if they promote a healthy attitude or physical well-being. However, such instructions often work more slowly than more narrowly focused approaches. Thus, it may be preferable to locate our obscurations in physical space and work with them more directly. For example, if we have obscurations related to hunger, it may be helpful to extend our capacity for feeling into our stomach. This is especially true if repression has caused us to move our awareness or energy away from the place of emotional discomfort.[24] In such cases, reversing repression often involves becoming aware of the parts of our body that have become energetically lifeless.

15. Empathy

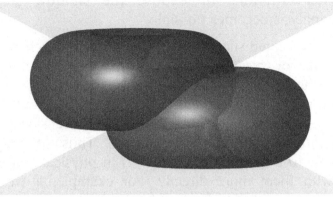

Figure 15: Empathetic energy.

15.1 *Empathy*

Empathy is defined as the ability to understand and feel the emotions of another. It is crucial to embodying the Physical Model, within which failing to feel the emotions of another person in physical space entails lacking some insight into reality.

Empathy is often easier in theory than in practice because we have limited access to the subjective view of others. For example, we might empathize with our brother, but when anger arises, our mind retracts rather than expanding to encompass his point of view. Even when anger is not present, a stranger may not rouse any empathetic concern in us simply because we are busy with something else. However, developing the empathy necessary for equanimity is impossible if we do not adopt a balanced and allocentric view rather than an unbalanced and egocentric view.

15.2 *Universal Empathy*

The following points form a very rough outline of an argument that humans are empathetic by nature. It relies on the fact that empathy is required for knowing (and vice versa), and implies that correct understanding leads to ethical action.

- The nature of humans is knowing.
- The fulfillment of that knowing nature is omniscience.
- Omniscience can only be achieved by a mind which knows everywhere and everywhen.
- A mind can only know multiple things at once in virtue of concepts that are emotionally or energetically charged.[25]
- Therefore, emotion must exist everywhere and everywhen in order to be omniscient.

Expressed more simply, omniscience requires universal empathy (and vice-versa). As it is our nature to know, it is also our nature to be empathetic.

Exercise: Feeling

Feel the world,
being aware of the location of those feelings.

Feel joy wherever it is easiest
and then increase that joyful space
by breathing into any forgotten spaces.

Feel your perceptions and thoughts.

Your mind may be pushed and pulled
by various contents of awareness;
try not to react, as action interferes with feeling.

PART V

BODY

To facilitate embodiment, it helps to develop a model of how the physical body feels rather than a model of how we conceptually know the body. This task is particularly important if the feeling of the physical body is difficult to express, in which case we may be prone to confuse these different notions of body.

16. Karma

Figure 16: Karmically connected worldlines.

16.1 *The Theory of Karma*

Karma is a Sanskrit word that is often translated as "causality" or "action". However, karmic connections are bidirectional, and karmic effects can be instantaneous, so karma cannot be mediated via causality in the traditional sense. Here, the meaning of the term karma is a blend of its traditional use in Indian philosophy with the idea of bidirectional causality.

In spiritual contexts, karma often refers to a moral law within the universe that rewards good behavior and punishes bad behavior. Regardless of whether karma results in any *physical* consequences for various actions, there are undeniable *psychological* consequences for thinking or acting in unbalanced ways. Therefore, a distinction is drawn between these two karmic mechanisms: psychological karma is a connection at the mental level that involves the nervous system, while physical karma is a connection at the bodily level that is mediated by external objects. The distinction between psychological and physical karma should probably be seen as gradual since they are somewhat inextricably linked (as described in *Section 8.4: Temporal Consistency*).

16.2 *Psychological Karma*

Psychological karma is synonymous with psychological conditioning or stimulus/response learning. For example, if a bell rings every time we are about to eat ice cream, the bell becomes a *conditioned stimulus* for ice cream. As the association of the bell with the ice cream is strengthened, a karmic connection is created between us and the bell. Although that does not seem like an inherently bad thing, the tendency of karma to disrupt equanimity can be quite serious, as when developing strong karmic associations with toxic stimuli produces addiction. In fact, even good karma is problematic, because karma of any kind can be antithetical to equanimity.

Psychological karma can be very subtle, and can even be caused by how we conceptually categorize the world. Consider the difference between different descriptions of the same event, such as "having breakfast" as opposed to "having a breakfast burrito with avocado, home fries, and sriracha". As such differences in conceptual spin have significant effects, it is important to be aware of the effects of categorizing events in different ways and viewing events from multiple points of view.

16.3 *Physical Karma*

Physical karma refers to the law of cause and effect, and may also involve some system of reward and punishment. It cannot be explained by the standard model of causality, since actions on entangled or karmically connected objects may instantly affect their entangled counterparts. It can be explained by bidirectional causality, but note that the common notion of karma does not specify its mechanism of operation (and neither has modern physics proven that entanglement operates on the worldlines of objects).

One way to think about physical karma is as something that extends our being discontiguously, as in quantum physics where entangled objects are described by a single description or system of equations. It can also be seen as the realization that our past and future continually affect us, just as we affect and are affected by objects to either side of us in physical space. Regardless of how we describe it, if we affect and are affected by the karmic connections that we make, then we should reject any models of ourselves as isolated and only adopt models that portray us as connected within a high-dimensional context.

16.4 *The Witness Model*

The Witness Model entails that we can observe phenomena without interacting with them. It models perception as a one-way process that is directed toward a witness, and disregards any reverse or two-way connections that occur between the subject and object.

Witnesses are considered impartial if they do not contribute to the interaction with the witnessed object. If all interactions are bidirectional interactions at the physical level, however, then it is impossible for a witness to perceive without having any effect on the witnessed object. Since the Witness Model reinforces the belief that experiments can be entirely unbiased, or that events can be perceived without the perceivers being even partially responsible for the outcome, it is at best a partial model of reality.

The notion that a witness can be entirely passive is reinforced by the theory of unidirectional causality, and therefore should be reevaluated if causality always involves bidirectional connections between events. If causality is bidirectional, then events such as going to a coffee shop should not be understood as merely going and hearing something or seeing something and returning with new memories and a more caffeinated body. In addition to those changes, we create a karmic connection with the coffee shop. Although we may not understand the intricacies of that karmic connection, we and the coffee shop become part of a larger whole, and share some degree of common fate from then onward.

17. What is the Body?

Figure 17: The body as a bundle of strings.

17.1 *Dimensionality and Contiguity*

There are two distinctions that help us to talk about the different notions of body that we might feel. The first is the distinction between the 3-D body and the multidimensional body that contains the 3-D body as a part. The second is the distinction between the contiguous body and the karmic (or discontiguous) body that contains both the body and all objects that are karmically connected or entangled with that body. Combining these distinctions gives rise to four different notions of body: the 3-D body, the multidimensional body, the 3-D karmic body, and the multidimensional karmic body.

The 3-D model of the body is our usual understanding of our body at the present moment. The multidimensional body is analogous to a string or worldline, and contains the 3-D body as a part. The 3-D karmic body contains both the 3-D body and all other 3-D objects with which it is entangled. Finally, the multidimensional karmic body contains all of the other notions of body.

The karmic body can be visualized as a rope that contains numerous entangled strings or a karmically connected bundle of worldlines. The strings that compose the rope come together to constitute our contiguous body and eventually separate back out. This weaving process occurs throughout the length of the rope, so in this sense the model of a rope does not fit: most ropes are not interwoven throughout their length. Thus the karmic body, besides being that rope, includes each of the strings that is entangled with it, and every string that is connected with those strings, *ad infinitum*.

17.2 Direct Perception

The theory of *direct realism* states that things are known directly, whereas *indirect realism* states that things are known indirectly, as by representations. The theory of indirect realism and the theory of mental representation that often accompanies it are embedded so deeply within our culture that direct realism is difficult to comprehend. How could there be direct connections between spatially separated subjects and objects?

Closely related to the theory of direct realism is the theory of *direct perception*, which may be understood as a form of knowing that is mediated by physical contact. Physical contact should be understood very generally in this case: if one string of our bodily rope is a photon that has bounced off of a table, then that photon serves as an (active) physical connection with the table. Thus, if it is possible to know in virtue of being, then we may know the table in virtue of that photon being a material part of us.

18. Where is the Body?

Figure 18: The body within an extended here-and-now.

18.1 *The Body in Spacetime*

The typical notion of the 3-D body is not an excellent model for the self; it is an abstraction that should not be reified. It implicitly cuts off the connection with the past and future that occurs when seeing the body as multidimensional (i.e., at least 4-D). But if the 3-D model of objects is not accurate, then it is a bit of a puzzle why humans use it. One possibility is that it is due to a limit of the geometry of language, which often models noun phrases as 3-D (or spatial) and verb phrases as 1-D (or temporal). However, that limitation of language is probably a result of the limited capacity of human visualization: humans cannot visualize 4-D objects at one time, even though we are such objects (see *Section 11.4: The Nervous System Model*).

If we see the past and future as fixed and causally inert, it may not make much of a difference to our lives to think of our body as 4-D. But if the past and future are causally efficacious and alive, then our body has living roots in both its past and future karmic connections. Significantly, abandoning the model of a past that has been left behind inevitably leads us to behave differently. Even if we are not able to say exactly *how* we are different in virtue of connecting with other worldlines, it is valuable to know that differences have been and will continue to be made in virtue of such connections.

18.2 *Where Am I?*

The karmic body is not narrowly localized in the here-and-now: our karmic body is partially inside of our skins and partially somewhere else. Thus, the question of where and when we exist in spacetime is not *simple*: different parts of us exist in different places and times. For example, the temporal interval within which we physically exist is equivalent to the length of our worldline. However, as we comprise multiple worldlines that correspond to multiple parts of our body or even different possible versions of ourselves, that length does not correspond to the measure of a single worldline between our birth and death.

Existing at different times may seem perplexing since it is not clear how we can move our body in the past and future. However, most of us believe that moving our body in the present will result in a different bodily location in the future, so perhaps our movement produces a different bodily location in the past in exactly the same way. Note that in both cases, the movement does not create an eternal change as it is partially determined by interactions with other worldlines in the past and future.

18.3 *Ethical Consequences of Location*

Extending the conceptual size of our mind or body may result in substantial moral changes, since even selfishly taking care of an extended self results in better behavior (i.e., due to that larger sphere of self-care). By holding all possible subjective perspectives, selfishness is transcended completely, and we naturally treat others with kindness.

In addition to the ethical consequences of clarifying where different parts of us exist, there are significant (karmic) ramifications to clarifying *when* we exist. In particular, seeing the past as causally efficacious establishes symmetry with the future, and implies that the end does not justify the means any more than the means justify the end.

Exercise: Being

Benefit all beings, including yourself.
Allow those actions to soften your boundaries.

Remain completely still in one place,
and drop any mental or emotional activities
that interfere with simply being.

Travel to various places, and make
mutually beneficial karmic connections.

PART VI

CONCLUSION

If our self-model has changed, then realizing those changes requires us to practice. The mind, emotions, and body each require different types of practice: the mind requires modeling, the emotions require meditating, and the body requires embodying.

19. Next Steps

Figure 19: The beginning of a worldline.

19.1 *Model*

The Subjective Model contextualizes the view from the here-and-now in a multidimensional space. It analyzes reality into three aspects: a mental aspect that is structured with references, an emotional aspect that is structured with energies, and a physical aspect that is structured with parts and wholes. The Physical Model is a combination of all possible subjective models and is therefore the view from everywhere and everywhen. As it construes the world as inherently meaningful, it is a view which is likely to benefit the world and us personally.

That said, the models discussed in this work are intended to provide the basis for our own model, as the value of gnosis may be lost by adopting a model that has not been critically analyzed. Hopefully, they have also helped to elucidate the ways in which other people operate, since those are often as important.

19.2 Meditate

The body should be still and relaxed; it is hard to sufficiently emphasize the need to relax if our resting state is far from baseline. It might help to scan the body and the environment at the beginning for any signs of tension.[26] The muscles should be moved slightly while doing so. The body will almost certainly need to be pushed into alignment, which may take a while if awareness of posture is not a frequent practice.

The emotions should be open, kind, empathetic, and warm. As with the body, it may help to scan the environment to ensure that feeling is present in everywhere and everything. If it is not, breathe life into that space: the cultivation of equanimity requires circulation. Emotions can be very subtle, so even if the emotions feel balanced, try to be aware of pervasive moods.

The mind should know or recognize what it is seeing. It is unnecessary to focus on any object or concept to the exclusion of others, unless perhaps the mind is jumping about. No thinking: if thoughts are occurring, try listening harder or seeing harder. If that doesn't work, analyze why the thought keeps recurring to develop insight into the source of the unbalanced cognition. Thinking is not bad, but it is good if you can periodically refrain from it.

The nervous system should be so still that it does not pull awareness away from being conscious of the body. If that causes sleepiness or boredom, then there is not enough appreciation for what is happening: take a nap or consider the benefits of practice. If open awareness causes the mind to wander, try directing awareness to the breath. Make sure all of the senses are open, but do not let the awareness wander exclusively to external objects.

Finally, if all of this is easy to do, continue practicing while walking about. If attraction or aversion arise in response to encountering some object, acknowledge and balance that feeling. At some point the practice itself is a greater obstacle than the obstacles it is designed to remove, and you can let it go.

19.3 *Embody*

Karma can be understood psychologically, so maintaining mental equanimity is an important step in being free of that karma. However, karma is also physical. Thus, it is beneficial to develop physical karmic connections with positive influences, as by decorating frequented places with enjoyable physical references and keeping them clear of unpleasant physical references. However, don't overdo it: you should also enjoy the opportunity to be someone else's karmic upgrade.

No matter how the result of your action appears from your point of view, it is impossible to know how that action may change the future or the past, or to know the ripple effects that those changes will have. Therefore, complete your actions with the aspiration:

May it benefit all beings.

Appendix A

Spacetime Diagrams

The diagrams in this book are based on spacetime diagrams, which are 2-D diagrams where the horizontal dimension represents space and the vertical dimension represents time (the future is up). All events within spacetime are volumes that have both a spatial and a temporal extent.

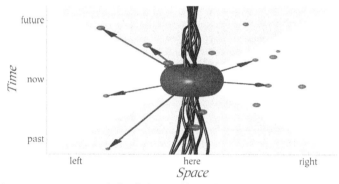

Figure 20: A model of the self within a spacetime diagram.

The vertical lines are called *worldlines*: they represent the course of a particular object (or world) in spacetime. In this work, worldlines are used to represent the 4-D body of an observer, while multiple worldlines can be used to represent a 5-D body (where the fifth dimension corresponds to probability). The grey triangles intersecting in the middle of Figure 20 locate the here-and-now at the center of the diagram (in physics, they represent light cones). The small spheres throughout the graph represent various events; for simplicity, their worldlines are omitted.

There are at least two objects in Figure 20 which are not present in traditional spacetime diagrams: *mind* and *emotion*, both of which are only illustrated only at the here-and-now since representing mind and emotions throughout the body's worldlines would make the diagram overly complex. The mind is represented by the referential arrows centered at the subjective origin, and emotion is represented by the torus in the same location. There is not too much significance to the fact that it is a torus, but I like that it connotes both fusion reactors and donuts (I am a big fan of the Simpsons).

Appendix B
Related Work

There are many parallels between this work, Indian philosophy, Tibetan Buddhism, Western cognitive science, and physics. Those with similar backgrounds have probably been able to infer the connections, but they are mentioned here explicitly in case you would like to learn directly from the (often more eloquent) source material that I learned from.

First, my formal education led to degrees in psychology, computer science, and electrical engineering. Most of my professional work is in computer science. I have studied philosophy and religion for many years, I dabble in popular physics, and enjoy Buddhism. I am not an excellent meditation practitioner and I don't have any authority to say exactly what Buddhism is, but much of this work derives from my understanding of Indian and Buddhist cognitive science.

The analysis of the self is common to several psychological and spiritual traditions. The term *gnosticism* refers to an ancient form of both Judaism and Christianity, although gnosis more generally refers to the development of self-knowledge as a means of spiritual transformation. Self-knowledge is also a key component of Buddhism, which denies the existence of a self and also highly recommends looking for that non-existent self. In fact, the practice of self-inquiry led to several of Siddhartha Gautama's key teachings.

Several insights about space presented in this book are present in much older works. Aristotle Stagiritis observed that, "Everything that exists must be in some place and occupy some room, and that what is not somewhere on earth or heaven is nothing"; see Cornford (1935, Timaeus

52b). This entails, among other things, that absolutely everything can be visualized. Immanuel Kant held that space and time are aspects of a mental framework by which we understand the events of the world. More poetically and perhaps more practically, Longchen Rabjam is famous for metaphors likening the nature of mind to space, and upheld a tradition that emphasizes spatial cognition as opposed to abstract thought.

The notion of karma that is developed in this work derives partly from Indian philosophy and partly from physics. The belief that karma works via retrocausality is my own hypothesis, although I am probably not the first person to come up with it.

There are several Sanskrit terms that correspond to central themes of this book. *Karma* was used untranslated. The *koshas* may be understood as precursors of referential levels. Finally, the analysis of emotions derives fairly directly from both the Sanskrit language and Buddhist theory, where emotional energy corresponds to *prana* and obscurations correspond to *kleshas*.

The Whole Part

This work is a departure from *The Whole Part* (Rogers, 2020) in several important respects.

One of the biggest simplifying assumptions is the replacement of various kinds of mental entities (i.e., percepts, concepts, and symbols) with the single term *concept*. Hopefully this will not be confusing to people who have read the previous work, as it will certainly be less confusing to people who have not.

Also, this work is considerably more broad in scope. The previous work was very cognitive: its treatment of emotions was cursory, and its model of the body was seen primarily through a cognitive lens. Unfortunately, using a mental model to understand the world may severely limit how the world is experienced. I'm not certain that there were any invalid statements in the previous work, but the presentation was unfortunately incomplete, and I am sorry if that omission perpetuated any confusion.

In more detail, the use of references in the previous work was primarily limited to *unidirectional* references, which makes it more likely to neglect the bidirectional aspect of physical interactions. While unidirectional references can offer a decent model of unembodied cognition, as when two people look at each other and only one person has an awareness of the other, the physical world is composed of interactions that are bidirectional and almost always symmetric (see the discussion in Price, 1996). So the physical aspect of the interaction where one person perceives another involves a symmetric karmic connection that may be overshadowed by a unidirectional model. That overshadowing is particularly significant if the bidirectional effect is non-trivial, and it often is: when you look at something, and maybe even when you think about something, a resonance is established with that thing which affects both connected objects.

Notes

[1] Three maxims are carved in the temple at Delphi: *know thyself, nothing in excess,* and *surety brings ruin.*

[2] This unitary view of the self is similar to the theory in Nyaya philosophy that the self is singular, permanent, and independent.

[3] The assumption of temporal directionality imposes additional complexity that should be avoided according to the principle of parsimony (i.e., Occam's razor).

[4] Physics itself is somewhat ambivalent: electrons can be represented as either continuous matter waves or discrete particles with a probability distribution.

[5] Mathematically, the light switch will have flipped an infinite number of times within that minute, but the series converges since the time that it takes to flip the switch is decreasing proportionately.

[6] Point-free topologies avoid this paradox by treating infinity as a process that can never be actualized. Aristotle is one of many philosophers to hold this view of *potential infinity*; see Tiles (2004).

[7] Point-free topologies are consistent with the axiom that any part always exists in the same number of dimensions as its whole, and thus entails that points cannot be parts of real objects; see Rogers (2020).

[8] Neglecting any friction on the table and numerous other complicating factors.

[9] In other words, a more relativistic model would not privilege a particular reference frame (even though there may be practical reasons for doing so).

[10] Since causes and effects imply both the act of making something happen and a temporal order, the more symmetric phrase "karmic connection" is used in place of "bidirectional

causal connection".

[11] People who think that changing the past borders on magical thinking often have somewhat homogenous responses: "The past happened and you can't change it, but the future can be changed because it hasn't happened". In both cases, the argument is just an appeal to a past or future existence (or lack thereof) that may not be fixed and which cannot be observed or verified.

[12] Our memories represent what happens after a certain event but not what happens before a certain event. Interestingly, some studies of memory consolidation show that our memories are replayed in reverse during sleep, which may help us to form symmetric representations of spacetime even though our travels involve only moving forward.

[13] I do not deeply understand the details of particle physics, so this is merely an intuitive conjecture.

[14] In more technical terms, the boundary can be seen as a linear separating hyperplane. Gardenfors (2004) presents a related theory that concepts are represented by convex regions.

[15] From a religious point of view, the proposal that the world is a mind is similar to pantheism, which holds that god is everything and god is conscious.

[16] Proponents of the no-ground view include the Madhyamika school of Buddhism, which argues that any model that includes a non-referential aspect of reality such as a ground consciousness (*alaya vijnana*) is only relatively true.

[17] "Mind" is often confused with "brain" if it is studied at all, because subjectivity is a problematic topic for the scientific method. However, the dual location of subject and object, or the *place* and the *base* of consciousness, has been a topic of debate since early Indian philosophy (see Ganeri, 2012).

[18] More specifically, the perceptual mind extends as far as sensation, and the conceptual mind extends even further.

[19] The terms "representation", "reference", and "reflection" are used synonymously in this work.

[20] These notions are also reflected in the laws of ownership as they pertain to material property and intellectual property.

[21] For example, what would it look like if the location of the first person pronoun referred to the location of awareness rather than the location of the body?

[22] These instructions are similar to a Buddhist meditation practice known as *the Four Foundations of Mindfulness*.

[23] Specific things are absolute and material, while generic things are relative and ideal. In Western philosophy, specific and generic things are called particulars and universals, respectively.

[24] Whether that's Buddhist repression that involves moving energy into the central channel, or Christian repression that moves energy into the sacrum, or Freudian repression that moves energy into the head, in all cases there may not be sufficient energy at the location of the klesha to purify it.

[25] While the analytic or rational mind may know something that is not emotionally charged, it cannot know multiple things at once.

[26] This meditation guidance summarizes my own practice, on a good day: I encourage you to read other sources and connect with a teacher if possible, since I am more of an academic than a practitioner.

Glossary

Awareness: Awareness is the subject/object knowing of the mind, which is produced by being conscious of references.

Body: Body is the *being* aspect of a self, which is structured using parts and wholes. Physically, it is analogous to matter.

Boundary: Boundaries are nominal objects that define the shape of actual objects and have an extent of zero along the dimension which they divide. Therefore, boundaries create parts that are connected. For a more substantial discussion, see Casati & Varzi (1999).

Consciousness: Consciousness refers to non-dual or reflexive knowing (i.e., of the body).

Emotion: Emotion is the *feeling* aspect of a self, which is structured using various potential and kinetic energies. Physically, it is analogous to energy.

Emotional energy: Emotional energy refers to the energy underlying emotions and is analogous to the Sanskrit term *prana*.

Karma: The Sanskrit term *karma* is used in this work to mean a type of causation that encompasses both causality and retrocausality. It may or may not have a moral component; see *Section 16: Karma*.

Mind: Mind is the *knowing* aspect of a self, which is structured using references. Physically, it is analogous to connections between events.

Model: This book describes several informal models of how things work: Lump, Map and Vehicle, Rug, Billiards, Connectionist, Witness, String, Subjective, Objective, and Physical.

Obscuration: Obscurations are poisons that turn emotional energy into toxic emotions. In Sanskrit, obscurations are called *kleshas*.

Reference: A reference is a thing that symbolizes or denotes a referent. For example, concepts are references to objects. References can be unidirectional or bidirectional, although symmetric references are better referred to as connections.

Referential level: Referential or epistemic levels are layers of cognitive references such that each layer consists of references to the previous layer; for more information, see Rogers (2020). The precursors of referential levels in Hindu philosophy are called *koshas*. They are similar to the five aggregates that Siddhartha Gautama found when he investigated the self.

Retrocausality: Retrocausality is the term for causation that works backwards in time.

Satchitananda: *Sat-Chit-Ananda* is a term denoting the nature of absolute reality dating back to the Upanishads. *Sat* corresponds to being or body, *chit* to knowing or mind, and *ananda* to peace or bliss. These aspects may also relate to the aspects of the body-as-experienced: *nadi, bindu,* and *prana*.

Self: A person's self refers to their self-concept or their identity.

Space: In this work, space is a generic notion that may be multidimensional and can correspond to physical space, conceptual space, or both.

Spacetime: Spacetime is the word coined by physicists for the 4-D space that combines 3-D (physical) space and 1-D time.

Toxic emotions: Toxic emotions are the result of combining obscurations with emotional energies.

Bibliography

Abbott, E. A., & Stewart, I. (2008). *The annotated flatland: A romance of many dimensions.* New York, NY: Basic Books.

Casati, R., & Varzi, A. C. (1999). *Parts and places: The structures of spatial representation.* Cambridge, MA: MIT Press.

Cornford, F. (1935). *Plato's Cosmology.* New York: The Liberal Arts Press

Ganeri, J. (2012). *The self: Naturalism, consciousness, and the first-person stance.* Oxford, United Kingdom: Oxford University Press.

Gärdenfors, P. (2004). *Conceptual spaces: The geometry of thought.* Cambridge, MA: MIT Press.

Kant, I., & Meiklejohn, J. M. D. (1990). *Critique of pure reason (Book 2).* Buffalo, NY: Prometheus Books.

Price, Huw (1996). *Times arrow and Archimedes' point.* New York: Oxford University Press.

Rogers, A. (2020). *The whole part.* Retrieved from https://thewholepart.com

Rucker, R. v. B. (1983). *Infinity and the mind: The science and philosophy of the infinite.* Canada: Bantam Books.

Thakchoe, S. (2017). *The theory of two truths in India.* In E. N. Zalta (Ed.), The Stanford Encyclopedia of Philosophy (Spring 2017). Metaphysics Research Lab, Stanford University. https://plato.stanford.edu/archives/spr2017/entries/twotruths-india

Tiles, M. (2004). *The philosophy of set theory: An historical introduction to Cantor's paradise.* Mineola, NY: Dover Publications.

Made in the USA
Middletown, DE
27 November 2022